CONTENTS

Introduction	3
Hidden Thoughts Produce Visible Results	7
She Forgave	12
Secret Power of the Dream Board	18
The Reverse Engineer	20
How to Decree a Thing	29
The Snake in the Grass	33
Thoughts/Inner Conversations	37
Magic	43
The Source of Problems	46
Imagination and Astral Travel	48
Seven Day Ultimate Challenge	51

INTRODUCTION

One of the greatest secrets in the world is that it is the human being's imaginatory faculty that powers and creates the events of his or her life. Secrets of the Imagination is a collection of stories that reveal this amazing yet hidden power. Between these pages we uncover the real secret to the the Law of Attraction.

What is that secret? The real secret of the Law of Attraction is this: What you imagine and feel...comes to pass. That's right. What you think about and add feeling to, hardens into real life experiences. It has nothing to do with affirmations, positive thinking, hypnotizing yourself, mantras, yoga etc... Simply stated; Imagining creates your reality.

And what that means for you and me is this...

We have to account for every single thought that passes through the gates of our imagination.

"Every single thought?" you ask.

Yes. Every single thought.

It's a frightening prospect to consider that our thoughts are creative. It's even more frightening to think that our feelings are creative. The plain truth is that both are true. Our thoughts and feelings (when combined), create or attract their physical equivalents to us here in our day to day lives. (You will hear this repeated in multiple ways throughout the book.)

Good News
◆◆◆

The Good News is this. As you read, you will:

- Learn several powerful techniques that you can use right away for material and spiritual benefits.
- Quickly understand the method to manifest all of your dreams.
- Immediately realize the simplicity of changing your entire situation from one of lack and unhappiness to one of abundance and joy.

Moreover, you will find these techniques easy to apply, not difficult. With repetition, they will become enjoyable and even pleasurable. Continue in their practice and you will discover a whole new world of power has opened up to you.

You will notice a connection between every imagination technique in this book. That is because every technique is attempting to help you do the same thing. Namely, take hold of your imagination and guide it with purpose.

Your thoughts and feelings have to match your aim in life. Meaning, you have to travel to that place in your imagination where your dreams and goals are a reality. For example, is there something you want to do? Someone you want to be? Somewhere you want to go? Well, your day to day habitual thoughts and feelings must match what it is that you want.

So let's assume I already know what I want. Let's say, for example, I wanted to live in a beautiful new home in a certain neighborhood. Once I'm sure that I really want this thing, I go to work. Not work like going to the office or factory or some other job. I go to work in my imagination.

Here's What I Would Do:

Now I know I want this home, so I go into some place that is quiet and private. It is a place that I use when I do not want to be disturbed. (You must find your own special place.)

I personally go into my private office at a time when no one will disturb me. You may find laying in bed at night is the best place for you. Anywhere private that you can close your eyes, relax, and speak freely without fear of being heard by those around you will work. Imagine that it is a place you would feel comfortable going to pray.

The next step is to enter into a special mood or feeling. Begin to think about what it would FEEL like if suddenly the home you wanted were yours RIGHT NOW. Like, **right now** someone just handed you the keys and said "This is now your new home."

For you, it might feel like winning the lottery. It's like an "Oh-My-God." feeling. It's the feeling you would have when you say loudly and with feeling "YES!" Take a minute or two to work your emotional self up and literally generate that feeling in your imagination. Do it now! You can do it!

Now carry that feeling with you and with eyes closed, mentally look at your home. Imagine that you are now living in it. It's your dream house! It's your beautiful amazing home. You live here. It's so awesome now. Everything worked out miraculously.

Think of your family and friends. You can imagine them in your home as well. Everyone is acting naturally. You can see all of your furniture and everything is so nice and it's really just perfect and it feels really good to be here. Feel how lucky you are! Feel so very fortunate! Feel thankful! Feel thrilled!

The key is to **be here now** in this place. Imagine being in your new home as if it were happening right now.

Ok. Take a some time to enjoy it. Let your emotions run wild for a minute (or minutes) until they begin to naturally come down from the rollercoaster ride you just took. A sense of satisfaction will come over you. As your mood begins to calm down, you should just relax and with eyes closed be quiet and rest in the silence. Breathe and know that what you just did was a powerful manifesting exercise. When you feel ready, open your eyes. Nice Work!

You may not know it now but what you just did was move a mountain. Stay with me here. I've got some tricks to teach you. Because it's time you know the truth. You have the power within you right now to attract anything you desire.

And while hidden from the uninitiated from time immemorial, these secrets are here within these pages revealed for you to use; You are cautioned however, to keep these methods a secret. Let their efficacy and potency be proved to you beyond any shadow of a doubt several times over.

Unfortunately, many whom you would love to share this fantastic discovery with will fail to believe you or even understand it. Have faith though. Be strong. There are many of us who, like you, have awakened to this great power. And we will all meet someday. Until then, good luck! And Happy Manifesting!

Blessings.

Walt

mentalscientist.com

HIDDEN THOUGHTS PRODUCE VISIBLE RESULTS

The Laboratory of Neuro Imaging at the University of Southern California suggests that the average human brain thinks as many as 70,000 thoughts per day or about 48.6 thoughts per minute. Now that's a lot of thoughts to be sure. Some wise people schooled in Secrets of the Imagination know that **our own thoughts which are hidden produce results that are visible.**

This knowledge can be exploited by you with miraculous results. Armed with this knowledge you can conjure up something amazing and miraculous for you and even for the loved ones in your life. Let's see what happens when one woman puts this idea into practice...

The Imagination Solves Problems

A woman named Lisa came to the Mental Scientist one day for a consultation. She was young, single, smart, and pretty. There was a problem, however. The women in her office were jealous of her and hated her. They were talking about her behind her back and seeking to get her fired.

Poor Lisa went home each evening in tears with deep feelings of resentment and anger. She couldn't believe that she was being treated in this way. What had she done to deserve this?
She began to hate her job and the other people in her office as well. To top things off, she was beginning to feel physically ill.

The Mental Scientist quickly diagnosed the problem. He explained to her how her inner feelings of anger and resentment had been present before the problems at work surfaced. He went on to say that the situation she was experiencing in her office was created by her own mind through the misuse of her own habitual thoughts and feelings.

This, she found hard to believe. She started to feel like she had come to the wrong person for help. She began to become angry, and desired to get up to leave, but something held her back. As shocking and weird as it sounded, there was a spark of Truth in his words. She needed to hear more.

After a further more complex explanation she wisely decided to follow the Mental Scientist's advise. He told her that he would give her a prescription that was sure to solve the problem. He wrote it out on a piece of paper. After a couple of minutes of writing, he stopped, put the pen down, and handed it to her.

He said to her "Read this out loud; slowly and with feeling." A bit confused, she looked at him and then at the paper. Suddenly it dawned on her. Looking down at the "prescription" in her hand, she began to read aloud slowly. It was a prayer. Names have been changed to protect identity. It went like this...

The Prescription

"To Miss Smith and all of the people in my office, I want you to know that I love you. I truly, truly, love you. You are all children of God and I love you dearly.

I now invite you into the theater of my mind. I want you to know that I see you and love you. In fact I now shower you with abundant love. I now and forevermore radiate to you the full and joyous love of the creator of life. I smile and give you a saturating and penetrating dose of the complete and never ending love of God. It consumes my heart and radiates from my being to you and to all in this office.

I bless this office and I bless everyone in it. This office is beautiful and is a wonderful place filled with the Joy and Love of God. It fills me with complete and immense joy and love to share the love of

God with you. God's love flows through me like a river that cannot be stopped.

Because I am filled with this immense love, those around me respond in kind. I get what I give. I give love, so I receive love in return. God loves me dearly and cares for me and will protect and love me forever. Thank you God for your eternal care and endless love of me. God is love and I am filled with the eternal love of God now and forevermore. Amen."

She was to read this prayer every morning slowly, meaningfully with a deep feeling of love and appreciation for God, for her own life, and for the people in her office. She was instructed that her prayer was not complete until a deep feeling of love and peace came over her.

If the deep feeling of love and peace did not come over her, she was to repeat the prayer with earnest sincerity until she "caught the mood." This she did, and soon, after each treatment she found herself feeling immensely better. As her inner mood changed towards the people in her office, at first she noticed nothing different on the outside.

Young Lisa, however began to enjoy her morning treatments. She found herself "getting lost" in the emotion of loving the people from her job and in her life. Her love prayer took on a whole life of its own and she began to spontaneously radiate love to everyone everywhere in her life each morning. Not only the people from her office, but other people from her life began to flash before her imagination and she would express her deep love for them as well.

As strange as it sounds she literally began to feel like she was bathing in the emotion of love. As she carried out her exercises, getting lost in the deep feeling of love, she found them to be the best part of her day because the emotion of love felt so good. She realized that love had been seriously lacking in her life; in her experience.

The best part is that the morning prayer sessions were beginning to have a lasting effect. The emotion and mood of love was seeping down into her subconscious. The "love sessions" as she came to call them were transforming her mentality. They were changing her on the inside, and spilling over to the outside. When she left her apartment each morning she felt like she was literally radiating love to everyone everywhere.

◆◆◆

What Happened?

The result was nothing short of a miracle. After two weeks of sincere morning prayers she received an urgent call from her sister. Their mother had fallen ill and she was needed at home in a distant city to help take care of her for an extended period of time. The office in which this young woman worked could not keep her position vacant and immediately fired her.

This did not bother her! Lisa was so full of love now. Her mentality had changed so much that she simply wished them well and moved home to take care of her mother. That following week in her home town she bumped into an old friend who mentioned that her office was looking for help. Lisa immediately applied and after a short interview was offered the job and at a much higher salary than she had been receiving in her previous position.

Her friend later told her that the people in the new office had simply *fallen in love with her*. She couldn't believe it. Before, it seemed that no one loved her; and now everything was different. In fact, now it seemed that everyone loved her. It was a huge blessing and some might have wondered how she had become so lucky. What was so different?

Deep in her heart, the young woman knew exactly what had happened. She had discovered something amazing about herself. She changed herself on the inside and the outside blossomed into the very same thing. From the Mental Scientist, she had learned an incredible secret.

"You get what you give." -Old Chinese Proverb

SHE FORGAVE

An acquaintance of mine (we'll call her Tina) once complained to me that someone at her place of employment was being mean to her. I was surprised to hear this as my friend always seemed to be on good terms with people in her life. I asked her to tell me more about the situation and here is what I found out.

In the office building where she worked there was a cafeteria. The cafeteria manager for some reason was being rude to her, oftentimes ignoring her and waiting on other customers instead of her. Strangely, this manager seemed to be nice and even extra friendly to other people, even going out of his way to please them. This baffled Tina and the situation was not only confusing, but it was making her angry, even to the point of tears.

She had never said or done a mean thing to this man and she wondered what she could have done to deserve such treatment. Things got so bad that now she was very uncomfortable every time she went to get lunch or a snack. After a while, she even began to avoid going to the cafeteria all together, oftentimes making up lame excuses to her coworkers as to why she couldn't join them for lunch.

I interviewed my friend for several minutes and after some gentle probing about the situation, confirmed something interesting about her. It was something that I already had suspected. When you have the Secret Key, you know that the outside experiences of our lives are equal what is going inside within our mental atmosphere.

In this business of solving our personal problems, realize that something does not happen to us out of the blue. Our inner seemingly hidden thoughts project themselves outwards to create our experiences. It is our inner thoughts and emotions, or the mechanism of our Imagination that constitutes the major creative influence of our outer affairs. It is, perhaps, Humanity's Deepest Mystery and has remained hidden from the majority of people. Therefore the name of this book Secrets of the Imagination.

Armed with this knowledge (that the inside equals the outside), I knew for sure that my friend was harboring some inner hostility toward someone or something in her life. This inner hostility or anger had surely manifested as this seemingly unrelated problem with the cafeteria worker at her job. Furthermore, I knew that if she had been full of love and on good terms with everyone in her life on the inside, it would have been impossible for her to experience discord with anyone or anything on the outside.

After some honest discussion, she courageously admitted to being very angry with a close family member. Several years earlier, her sister had lied, cheated and stolen her boyfriend away from her. As she related the story I noticed a change come over her body. A subtle hostility within her was coming to the surface as she spoke. Her face and hands became rigid,
her voice became harsh and her breathing was abnormally shallow.

As her eyes welled up with tears, it was clear that she had been harboring a secret hatred inside her heart. In this poor woman's experience, she had never forgiven her sister and it had become a hidden pocket of poison in her system. This un-forgiveness, (poison) sat like a disease in her mind and affected her every interaction with the people in her life.

I gently explained to Tina that we cannot hide what is inside our hearts, because the inside always and must express itself to the outside. In fact, when we view an individual and their physical or outer conditions or environment, we can report with remarkable accuracy on the condition of their mental and spiritual estate. While my friend Tina had been hurt and it was unfair what had happened to her, what she did not know was that she needed to completely forgive her sister on the inside and let go of the painful past in order to come into good terms with everyone and everything in the outer life.

After a thorough explanation of the hidden connection between the unforgiveness of her friend and her relations with everyone and everything in the world around her, she broke down and admitted that she knew how angry she was and that it had been something she just couldn't seem to let go of. She acknowledged her understanding of the link between her anger and how she was being treated by not only the cafeteria worker but everyone else in her life. As the wet tears streamed down her face, she saw a new light and admitted that she secretly suspected that she was responsible for what had been happening to her.

Seeing that she was now ready, I immediately prescribed an antidote to neutralize the poison. I wrote down a powerful remedy for her on a piece of paper with some important words which she was to repeat morning noon and night for several days. It was about a page long and went something like this:

> *My dear Sister…I love you. I remember the love we had growing up as young children. I remember all of the wonderful things you did for me and for all of the kindness you showed to me. I am so thankful for you and am thankful to God for allowing us to be together and to have this wonderful experience together.*

> *I wish you love and I wish you the greatest joy of life. I share your desire for the best and now call down from heaven all of the wonderful blessings of life for you and for all of the loved ones in your experience. I praise God for you and for your kindness. I praise God for blessing me in the most amazing ways. I praise God for forgiving me for harboring anger of any kind.*

I thank you God for forgiving me and filling my heart with unspeakable love and joy. Sister...I know that this experience may have caused you some fear, anxiety, or possibly some form of guilt. I want you to know that it is ok to let it go. I completely and lovingly forgive you and set you free. You are a child of God and God's eternal love surrounds you saturates and blesses and comforts you. I too am surrounded by the love and eternal blessings of God. We now and will forever grow and live under His almighty protection and love.

Thank you dear sister for your wonderful love and kindness. My love for you overflows like a beautiful waterfall. I praise God for you and for the gift of life. May God bless you, prosper you, and keep you safe. I love you so, so, so, dearly. I love you so very dearly that words cannot convey. I love you so dearly.

I thank you God for releasing me and for filling me with complete and abundant love. I can feel this enormous love overflowing from my heart and flooding into all of my life and experiences. My entire heart is now saturated with abundant Love for everyone and everything, everywhere.

Thank you, thank you, thank you, thank you! Thank you God. Thank you Heavenly Father. I love you. I love you. I love you. I love you. I love you. I love you. I love you. I love you. I love you. I love you. I love you.

(repeat as needed)

◆◆◆

This prayer ultimately transformed her mind. As she repeated the prayer slowly, lovingly and feelingly each day, it seeped down into her heart and changed her life. It released the evil from her heart. It cleansed the poison from her mind and allowed her to truly and completely forgive her sister.

The conclusion to the story was nothing short of a miracle. A few short weeks later I met again with Tina. She reported feeling an unspeakable peace inside her heart. She felt that God had come back into her life and that the love she was now experiencing had turned her into a very grateful person. I never asked her about the cafeteria worker issue and we agreed that she would continue her prayer treatments and to meet up again in another few weeks.

In the meantime, her daily prayers continued. A few weeks passed and we met again. By this time a big change seemed to have come over her. She reported with a smile that she was full of love in her heart.

Indeed as I looked at her, it was something that could be seen visibly, in her face and in her eyes. In fact several people had recently remarked to her at how wonderful she appeared. One person during the preceding week had actually told her she was beautiful. That had never happened!

Friends, family, and even strangers were beginning to become attracted to her in an amazing and wonderful way. The whole world was beginning to be kind to her as she had nothing against anyone but only love in her heart. Then one day a strange thing happened.

It occurred to her that the cafeteria person who had previously been so mean to her was absent and that she hadn't seen him in a while. She inquired with a coworker about his whereabouts.

What she told her nearly made her jaw drop.

Apparently he had already been gone for more than two weeks but she hadn't noticed. He had quit his position suddenly and left for another job in another location. Simply put, he was out of her life! When she told me about it, I smiled knowingly. I thought to myself, "This is Secrets of the Imagination 101. What a blessing."

She asked me why I was smiling. I looked at her carefully to be sure that she heard my words. I explained that it would have been impossible for him to be in her experience any longer. She was so full of love and forgiveness that it had completely overtaken her mentality; her personality had literally been renewed.

Tina's entire being was now overflowing with love and kindness. There was no room any longer in her life for anyone who could possibly treat her poorly. Her heart had been cleansed by a potent dose of Love. She smiled and understood. The secret miracle was no longer a secret to her.

SECRET POWER OF THE DREAM BOARD

As a teenager, young Candy loved to write all about her dreams and goals. All of the things she ever wanted to do and be she wrote in her personal journal. She described her dreams in detail and even pasted pictures of her ideal life inside the pages. After high school, Candy and her family moved and Candy's journal became misplaced. For many years her journal was thought to have been lost.

In the mean time, her life underwent many unexpected changes. She had to give up on her dream of attending University in order to take care of her father who was suffering from a long-term illness. As her life progressed, so many things happened that she would never have expected. During those times of seeming uncertainty and change, she never allowed her circumstances to get her down. Even though life didn't appear to be happening as she had dreamed about she always tried to stay positive and pursue opportunities that came her way.

Years later Candy sat quietly contemplating the strangeness of life. So much had happened since high school. After her father passed, she had met her future husband, got married and raised a family. And now, her parents were gone. Sadly the time had come to sell the old family home.

As she was cleaning out the family attic. She happened upon some dusty old boxes. Opening them up, Candy was astonished to discover her high school journal! There it was lying tucked away in a box with some other forgotten relics from high school. She was delighted.

Frantically, like a young schoolgirl, she opened it up and began to read. Candy couldn't believe her eyes. Turning each page slowly one by one, she began to read and smile to herself. There were so many pictures she had carefully cut out of magazines, the inspirational quotes, the goals; all of it came back to her and she remembered the hopes and dreams of her young former self.

But what made her almost faint was the fact that practically every dream, every goal that was listed in her journal…had somehow, mysteriously…

…Come true.

Yes, it's true. Against all odds, even though early on she had been forced to give up on the path she intended, things ended up working out anyway. When she was forced to give up on her plans of going to college to stay home and take care of her Dad, Cindy, being a very industrious young woman, started a home business. Over time, her internet enterprise grew and she was able to make a very good living with her online store.

Later, after her Father had passed, she met the man she would marry. He traveled a lot for work and ended up taking her literally around the world with him to all of the amazing places that just "happened" to be listed in her journal.

As she continued turning the pages she discovered a cut out picture of her ideal dream home from many years before. An eerie chill went throughout her body because the picture of the home in her journal was oddly similar to the one they had just closed on a few months earlier. The yard, the deck, even the siding, were nearly a match. She shook her head in amazement. It all seemed so impossible and yet here was the proof of some strange miracle.

Her forgotten dreams had all come true.

Note: If you too have a dream/vision board, be sure to put only the things on it that you truly desire. Remember that there is an incredible power within your imagination that will bring those coveted desires to you. You do not control the timing, but trust that in some mysterious way, it will all work out.

THE REVERSE ENGINEER

Brilliant scientists are able to take a finished product such as a piece of machinery and take it apart to see "how it works." Rather than starting at the beginning on the proverbial drawing board, they start at the end, take a product in its' finished state and work in reverse order to discover how it functions and ultimately how to build a new one. This process is called reverse engineering.

Your Imagination Can Work in Reverse Order As Well

It's true. We humans can use our imaginations to reverse engineer almost any situation we desire. We simply start with the finished product and work backwards. How does that work? Read slowly and consider this closely guarded secret.

There is a psychological law of being that goes like this…

If a happy situation creates a happy feeling…then the reverse is also true that……a happy feeling creates a happy situation.

Huh??? A happy feeling creates a happy situation?

That's right. You read correctly. You see, it works both ways; forward or reverse. So realize that you can engineer or create any happy situation you want simply by working in reverse order. Rather than waiting for a happy situation to come along and make you happy, reverse engineer a happy situation by imagining and indulging in the feelings of a happy situation.

You literally go to the end or start at the end; the finished product so to speak. The finished product being the happy feeling of some good thing happening. Basically you entertain the feelings of joy associated with something wonderful happening and the Law of Attraction does the rest to bring it to you.

Sound ridiculous? Of course it does! It is so ridiculous sounding, however, that most people would never suspect that it works and therefore it remains an incredible secret.

"But can it possibly be true?" you ask.

Do not just take my word for it. Prove it for yourself. We are going to use it right now in the following exercise to manifest something you want or need.

Caution: It sometimes works quite quickly.

Let's go down the proverbial Rabbit Hole. (Warning: This will require control of your imagination).

◆◆◆

Begin Manifestation Exercise

Step 1: Come up with something you want.
Is there something that you really want or need right now? Is it a good thing? Come up with one thing right now that you feel would make your experience a better one. It could be something you need or just something you've been wanting. Maybe a job, a car, a romantic partner, a house, a better relationship, pay a bill, etc.

Choose one. We will use it for the following manifesting exercise. Take five minutes to come up with your want. (start with something simple, yet important to you.)

Step 2: Go somewhere private and relax.
Ok, you know what you want. Now you will need a private, quiet place where you can go, relax, and create your final product. (Your final product being the feeling of your wish having already been fulfilled.) Consider this private, quiet, space your laboratory where you will engineer or reverse engineer as it is, your desired situation.

Get into a comfortable position such as in a soft reclining chair. Close your eyes and begin to relax. Let go of your worries and prepare yourself to use your imagination. You are going to create a scene in your mind of your wish having already come true. Allow yourself to really calm down, relax and get into the mood of what it would feel like if your desired situation has already come to pass in the here and now.

Step 3: Create your imaginary scene.
Now what would the scene look like if your desire came to pass? We know what it would feel like. Feel those feelings of your desire coming to pass now but also imagine what it would **look like**. What do you see? Are people congratulating you? Can you see a new car or a new house? Is someone promoting you? Are you looking at a huge bank balance? Imagine what you want to see! Imagine what you would see happen if this thing actually came true! Feel what you would feel if this thing happened!

Step 4: Enter the scene. Use all 5 senses if possible. See, smell, taste, feel, and hear! Enjoy it and experience it fully. Interact with the people you see. See and hear people telling you the things you what you want to hear. Smell and breathe the air in. Feel the emotion of your desire coming to pass as if it really in this moment just happened for you.

FEEL IT! It has happened! YES! Doesn't it feel incredible? Catch the mood of your dream coming true and build up the visual images. Allow the emotions to come to the surface and truly indulge yourself in the experience you have created for yourself.

The main idea here is to dive in and really feel the emotions. Feel, feel, feel it happening! Smile and enjoy your experience to the fullest. Allow yourself to feel really, really good. It's all happening...NOW!!!

After a few minutes, allow your mind to relax. If you have done your job well, you may feel a bit spent. You may also feel a sense of satisfaction; as if this thing actually happened. Your work is done for now. Later on, you are free to repeat the exercise as you feel the need to.

How do you know it is working? You will know it is working when you naturally begin to feel the emotion you would feel if your desire actually happened. There will be a sort of feeling of satisfaction that comes over you. Like when you release a huge sigh of relief and that feeling that everything is ok comes over you.

It is then that you know it is working. Carry that feeling with you keep it alive. Be confident. Be vigilant. In time, your desired state will be created on the outside, the same as you created on the inside.

How it happens from here is a bit of a mystery. You will find your imagination taking you on a journey across a series of events in your day to day life that will ultimately result in your dream becoming a reality. Do not worry. Do not be dismayed at what you see happening. Rather, have faith. Trust in your almighty imagination. It knows best.

Practice is important. Your results will continue to improve with practice so do not give up after the first exercise. The Imagination is like a muscle; it gets stronger the more you use it. Create a routine and make a habit of exercising your imagination in this way. The more you practice, the easier it will be to maintain the mood or feeling of the wish fulfilled and that is the secret to manifesting.

And take note of this important fact. The results you get may take some time. It could be a few hours, days, weeks, or months in some cases. On the other hand, some things will happen *almost immediately*. Don't worry about it. It all works out perfectly you will find.

Lastly: The results you get may not be 100% as you imagined. Trust that what happens will be just as wonderful or even better than your initial conception. So long as you are imagining good things that bring feelings such as Love, Joy, and Happiness, you will have nothing to worry about. More and more you will find yourself becoming surrounded by things and situations that elicit these emotions in you.

For now, it is not your job to try and figure out how these things will mysteriously come about. Just leave it to your Deeper Mind to take care of the details. It knows best and will take care of you. Remember, your imagination has mysterious methods of working that you are currently not aware of. Its' ways are past knowing.

This is a powerful secret. Keep it to yourself. Once this Truth sinks down into your mind. It will become clear that your Imagination is the hidden power that engineers or creates the events of your life.

> "Finally, brethren, whatsoever things are true, whatsoever things are honest, whatsoever things are just, whatsoever things are pure, whatsoever things are lovely, whatsoever things are of good report; if there be any virtue, and if there be any praise, think on these things."
>
> Philippians 4:8

◆◆◆

He Reverse-Engineered a Win at the Poker Table...

John Q. was invited to play poker with some new work friends. This all sounded good to John except for the fact that he was a terrible poker player. The sad truth was that every time he played poker, he lost. Pitifully, he started to really worry about the game. He was to the point of feeling physically sick.

What was supposed to be a fun evening with some friends would probably end up being an embarrassing disaster. He thought that it would be easier to just give the other players his money up front rather than lose it all a little at a time over the course of an evening. He was afraid that he would look stupid.

John began wondering what excuses he could make up to get out of going.

It was at that moment an old memory popped into his mind.

◆◆◆

The Imagination is a Helper in Time of Need

His friend had returned from the thrift store one day with a strange book. It was a really weird book claiming to have occult secrets inside. Inside was a strange imagination exercise that was referred to as reverse engineering.

The gist of it was that you were supposed to go somewhere quiet, silence the mind, and imagine the perfect outcome to any problem that was plaguing you. This imagination exercise, according to the book, had the power to actually change the outcome of so many problems that bother us. At the time, John had understood the concept but never took the opportunity to put it into practice. "Now." he thought to himself. "What do I have to lose? I will try it today."

And so, with nothing to lose, John did exactly as the mysterious book recommended. That very afternoon, prior to the poker match, he went into a quiet, secluded place where no one would disturb him. He took the time to completely relax, silenced his mind, and then began to think about his new friends and the fun evening to come.

In his mind's eye he saw the other players. He looked around the room, and breathed in the imaginary air. After several minutes of quietly contemplating the scene it all started to take on a *feeling of realness*.

He infused the imaginary scene with happiness and he began to feel the happiness of sitting at the table with his new friends. All of the former anxiety melted away as he got into the mood of spending time here in this new situation. He saw the smiles and laughter, the food, the friendly conversation, and yes, the cards.

As he continued, he first tried to envision something simple. He wondered what it would feel like to simply win one hand in the game. He saw himself holding the winning cards and then showing it to the table. He heard the congratulations of the other players. He even pictured pulling in the imaginary chips and stacking them up in front of himself. It was actually exciting and it felt really good.

In his imagination he actually began to experience the feeling of exhilaration. He continued his exercise and indulged himself in the feeling and tried to keep that feeling going like riding a wave on a surfboard. In the dark silence he was smiling. It was so wonderful having a winning hand and raking in the chips. It felt really good.

This exercise he continued for several minutes and after a while his subconscious mind began to relax. Inwardly he felt that he had done enough. He naturally stopped and rested quietly in the stillness. After several minutes of peaceful silence, he opened his eyes.

His subconscious mind responded in a very interesting way. John Q., after his mental exercise was completed, felt a sudden and compelling urge to research poker strategies. He got on the internet and for the next few hours became thoroughly engrossed in learning about poker. He couldn't tear his eyes away. He was fascinated. Within a short period of time he learned several key tips that would help him during the poker game.

Later that evening, he drove to his friend's house as planned. Before getting out of the car, he again began to feel nervous about the game. As he sat there, he simply closed his eyes, took some deep breaths and recalled the images and feelings of winning the game.

It was easy to do because he had already spent so much time earlier in the day fully indulging in the emotion. After a minute or two the joyful peace returned to him and he was confident once again. With a smile on his face he went inside and joined his friends.

◆◆◆

How it all unfolded...

The game lasted for hours. As the evening progressed, John's poker chip stack went up, it went down and then went up again. Through the ups and downs, John succeeded in maintaining his joyful demeanor.

When tempted to be afraid of losing his growing pile of chips he simply inwardly began to indulge in the joy of winning. He allowed it to wash over him as he played the game. It saturated his mentality as he played the hands and laid down his bets.

At the end of the evening, it may or may not surprise you to learn that he won the game. His heart was beating wildly as he raked in the winnings. His mind and body was overcome with what could be best described as a wave of gratefulness and adrenaline. Just as he had seen in his imagination, his friends smiled joyfully and congratulated him on his great poker skills.

Later, he got into his car to go home and for a moment sat quietly pondering the evenings' events. "How did I win?" he asked himself. "How could it be? I'm not usually this lucky." He smiled awkwardly.

In the silence, it occurred to him. A shiver went through his entire body. He realized the Truth of what had happened and was speechless.

It was something he suspected but yet could not get himself to believe, however now there was no other explanation. He understood finally that the winning of the poker match had occurred not this evening, but rather...

...earlier in the day when he had experienced it in his imagination.

"It's true," he thought to himself. Before he had even arrived at his friends home to play poker, he had already won. The event of winning had already been processed in his consciousness where there was no opposition. Winning at cards was an event that had already been pre-built into his mentality.

He knew it was true but stunned all the same. As he sat there, a feeling of loneliness and sadness washed over him as he realized that there was no one he could talk to about what had happened. No one would believe him. They would think him to be mad.

But that was no matter. That evening's events marked a turn in John Q's life. He experienced a walk on the mysterious side of life and the secret he learned there would change his outlook... forever.

As he drove home in the dark a quiet calm came over him and he began to feel better. A knowing smile crept over his face. His eyes were twinkling as he contemplated exactly how he had made contact with this strange, mysterious power deep inside of himself. "Things were going to be different from now on," he thought.

"What you see...is what you get."

-Flip Wilson

HOW TO DECREE A THING

The Greatest Secret is that the words you speak (even the words you speak inside your heart)...come true. You are the genie in the bottle. Not only the words you speak, but the thoughts you truly feel and believe to be true become an established part of your experience.

It is stated quite nicely in the Bible's by Book of Job.

He says:

> "Thou shalt also decree a thing, and it shall be established unto thee: and the light shall shine upon thy ways."
>
> Job 22:28

Stated in modern terms, what this means is: What you say...comes true.

Remember that **both our words *and* our thoughts** are the equivalent to our "decrees." The worst part of this Truth is that the bad thoughts we think and speak also have a tendency to be created or established in our experience.

The Bible also states clearly in the book of Matthew that we will have to account for "every idle word." Again, **both our words *and* our thoughts** can be included when we talk about our "idle words." That means we must pay attention to all of our words and thoughts for they are creative.

A surefire way to improve your situation from this day forward is to lose the habit of all negative thinking. Switch your thoughts to the things that are good for you and yours. Be positive in your mental outlook and in your verbal statements. Avoid listening to the negative statements of friends, family and strive to avoid all negative input of any kind from the television or other forms of mass communication.

While difficult at first, it will become easier as you create the habit of controlling your thinking. Once you recognize the link between what you have been imagining and feeling and your daily reality you will begin to make every effort to imagine the best. Very quickly, and as a matter of Law, miraculous changes and opportunities will manifest in your life.

This is the Greatest Secret and it has now been whispered in your ear. Think only about the wonderful things that are good for you; Think only of the beautiful, amazing things you want to have and happen in your life.

Also, keep it quiet for now. Spare yourself the negative feedback. It is now a part of your own secret knowledge. Smile, and use this power to build your life as you wish it to be. Your life starts a brand new chapter from this moment.

◆◆◆

He Decreed a Thing

One morning a man went out to start his car. It turned over but did not start. This was bad news because he would again be late for work for the third time in as many weeks. He was experiencing considerable stress as he did not have the money to repair his car. He was angry too. Why did he have to struggle when so many others had it so good?

As usual, his kind neighbor helped him with a jumpstart and he was on his way. The man knew, however, he would be needing help getting his car started all the time now. What he needed now more than anything was a simple vehicle that was reliable. Secretly, in his heart, he longed for the smell of a brand new model. Of course that could never happen as he was broke, and barely making ends meet as it was. He simply couldn't afford a new car.

The very next morning, it was bitterly cold outside. It was actually the coldest day of the year. The day's schedule at work was busy and he got up early to leave. Fearfully he turned the key on his ignition. Nothing. Frustrated and angry he was at the end of his ropes. Something had to change. This was not the way he wanted to live his life. He was constantly in fear, worried for his job, and broke.

He sat alone in his car, late for work, and as tears welled up in his eyes he decreed aloud "I want a new car, and I want one now!!! I'm tired of living like this and I simply must have a new car!!!" He yelled it out loud again; and then again. The neighbors must have thought he was crazy as he sat inside his heap of junk at six a.m. yelling at the top of his lungs.

◆◆◆

Miracles Come in Strange Packages

What happened next is quite interesting. Later that same day, on the way home from work, the man was turning into a gas station and another vehicle pulled out at the same time and smashed into his old car. His vehicle was heavily damaged but oddly, still driveable. He barely got it home, parked it and without thinking, began to walk.

He walked away from the car *with purpose* and continued walking, all the time decreeing out loud... "I must have it! There has to be a way!!!" "I must have a new car!" "This can not go on!" Several minutes went by and as he looked up, he realized he was walking in the direction of the car dealerships on the other side of town.

"Is it possible? Would they sell me a car?" he wondered. He had nothing to lose at this point. Maybe they would laugh at him, but he didn't even care anymore. He picked up his pace and kept going.

◆◆◆

What happened?

Fast-forward to a few short hours later, the man was driving a brand new car! It was one that was just perfect for him. "But how?" you ask. "He didn't have any money."

The story goes that the dealership was really motivated to sell to him because it had been so bitterly cold that week and very few customers had come out to buy cars. Even though he couldn't afford a large downpayment, with his good credit, and the insurance money he would receive from the *accident*, the dealership was willing to extend him the loan he needed to make the purchase.

He was so thrilled on his ride home. The new car smell filled his nostrils and as he pulled up and parked behind his old car. He took a few moments and sat inside thinking.

Why had he suffered for so long? Could he have had the car sooner? Earlier he was at the end of his ropes. Now here he was sitting in this brand new car. It smelled so good. He smiled, barely holding back the tears of gratitude, contemplating the strangeness of life. He never forgot the incident.

"Your Thoughts Move Mountains"

Walter Crosson

THE SNAKE IN THE GRASS

A man named Joe was having problems at work. He was suffering from a severe case of stress because he felt like he was being set up for failure by his incompetent boss. This boss had "thrown him under the bus" so to speak on numerous occasions making him appear untrustworthy and incompetent himself.

He actually had a bad reputation in Joe's office. Other people at the company often referred to him as "A snake in the grass." Most people tried to avoid working with him.

Meanwhile, an upcoming sales convention was worrying Joe's "snake in the grass" boss like nothing else. Big interests were flying in from around the globe. A lot of business was at stake for the company. There were deadlines that might not be met and the boss feared for his job.

Not surprisingly Joe was again being set up as the so called "fall guy" for the upcoming event. It looked like there was no way to win. His incompetent boss began tasking him with last minute responsibilities that were all but impossible to achieve. He realized that he was being set up for a huge failure and then possibly termination.

Joe, full of anxiety and at the end of his ropes, was referred by his friend to an "Imagination Expert" for a consultation. When Joe showed up in my office he appeared nervous, exhausted, and physically ill. We took some time to sit and calmly talk things over.

Over the course of several minutes he told me his story and after a while, he finally began to relax. I told him that I had a solution for him that was a bit unorthodox but that had worked for several people already. He seemed open to trying my remedy and so I continued.

I explained to him that one of the secret powers of his mind was to be able to guide or manipulate his imagination. This imagination, I explained, produced events in our own lives just as sure as the Sun rises and falls each day.

Though skeptical at first, Joe seemed to understand the concept and with some coaching on the sacred and mysterious art of inner thought manipulation, the solution became clear to him. Together we came up with a secretive yet potent plan with which to deal with the situation.

◆◆◆

The Mysterious Power That Works

The event was two weeks away and the solution to his problem began with a simple exercise. What was that exercise? Joseph was instructed to simply imagine the perfect solution or outcome.

Each morning when he woke up and prior to going to sleep in the evening, Joe slipped into a very relaxed state and quietly visualized or imagined for several minutes an absolutely wonderful event. He saw people walking up to him and sincerely congratulating him and thanking him for his good work. He put himself into the scene and actively enjoyed it as if it were really and truly happening.

Even during the daytime as he continued to work on the event details, if tempted to be fearful, he immediately went into a quiet place, reversed his thinking and focused on a fantastic outcome. Then things started to change…

Joseph began getting into the mood of a successful outcome and after several days of this exercise actually **began to really feel what it would be like** if everything worked out in a fantastic way. (That was how he knew that his exercises were working.) The results were astonishing.

Within a few days of practicing the mysterious exercises, Joe's boss was called out of town on an urgent family matter. On the outside, it looked like the worst had happened. Just as he had previously feared...everything fell into his lap and would certainly be a disaster.

Joe was stunned. He had become the ultimate fall guy. There would be no one else to blame but himself. Suddenly he was not only partially responsible for a successful conference, he was completely responsible.

He was immediately tempted to worry and throw in the towel, but then he remembered his exercises and wisely decided to focus on the positive outcome he desired. He retreated to his office, shut the door and relaxed his mind completely. He again visualized the perfect outcome and got in the mood of a great event coming off without any hitches or problems.

After several minutes **he succeeded in overcoming the fearful thinking** and suddenly a strange thing happened. A feeling washed over him and he realized that with his boss away, he was free to make decisions on his own, without interference. He could brainstorm and come up with unconventional solutions to make the event go off without a hitch.

More than that, some of Joseph's coworkers saw his unfortunate predicament and *were moved to help him*. No one wanted to see the so called "snake in the grass" boss win. Joseph was not alone! In fact, his office was full of people who were willing to pitch in and assist and over the next several days, everyone became so very helpful that Joseph was overcome with the feeling of thankfulness.

It was truly a miracle and the outcome was nothing short of amazing. The event ended up being a huge success and just as he had secretly imagined, the wonderful outcome came to pass. At end of the conference many people congratulated him and he was formally recognized by several higher up managers in the organization for his great work. Rumors were even spreading around the office that he was up for a big promotion!

Joe smiled with joy at having discovered a new yet hidden source of power. Never in his life had he dreamed such a power existed. He wanted to tell the world; but wisely kept it a secret.

Followup Note:

Joe was so impressed with his results that he incorporated a daily visualization routine into his life. Every morning and evening and even sometimes during the day at work (behind closed doors), he would do his imagination exercises; always getting into the mood or feeling of his wishes fulfilled.

After a couple of months another *miracle* happened. In a strange turn of events his "snake in the grass" boss was transferred to another department in the big company. Joseph was immediately promoted to take his place!

As Joseph sat looking out the windows from his new corner office, he was speechless. He was beginning to suspect that the world was nothing like he had once understood it to be. "Where to go from here?" he thought smiling to himself. He took out a notepad and begin to right down a list of some of the things that he really wanted in life.

> *"To bring anything into your life, imagine it's already there."*
>
> -Richard Bach

THOUGHTS/INNER CONVERSATIONS

I saw a fantastic science fiction movie several years ago and it so intrigued me that I've never been able to completely stop thinking about it. I realized why I was so fascinated by it a few years ago when I finally discovered the truth about the connection between our imagination and our realities.

The movie title is Sphere and was directed by Barry Levinson. It starred Dustin Hoffman, Samuel L. Jackson and Sharon Stone from Baltimore Pictures, 1998.

Briefly, it's about a team of scientists that discover a crashed spaceship resting at the bottom of the ocean. Inside the ship is a "Sphere." The scientists quickly learn that the sphere is causing their thoughts to come alive and manifest in real life. Chaos ensues when they begin to encounter their manifested thoughts.

It's a simple premise for a perfect sci-fi horror movie. How terrible it must be for these people to encounter all of their deepest fears, hurts, longings etc. I know I would hate to have to encounter some of the awful thoughts I've had in my life. I'm sure both you and I would rather avoid such a predicament.

But here's the truth. We are encountering, everyday, every moment, our spent thoughts. Look around you. Your entire situation is set up in a way that allows you to think your habitual thoughts day in and day out.

For example: are you an angry person? Not really a very angry person? Ok, you just get angry sometimes? If so, I bet there are just enough situations in your day or week that magically show up to allow you to express that anger and fulfill your habitual anger expression requirement.

Or how about this? Do you know someone that is always having trouble with people? Someone that is always being mistreated or disrespected by his or her peers; passed over for promotion, or any number of unfortunate examples?

Well, it's highly probable that this person is engaging in negative private mental conversations every day with these people. These conversations that take place in the imagination are reproduced by the mind and show up as real-life circumstances.

◆◆◆

The Example of Jon

For example, Jon Smith is in sales. He hates his job. He hates his boss. His boss is always saying things to Jon in front of other people that embarrass him. Jon's boss is always saying to Jon things like: "Your not doing a good job." "You screwed up again." "Why did you do it that way?" "We are not going to promote you." "Try to be more like XYZ person."

Every day on his way to work, Jon holds imaginary conversations with his boss. He is thinking the worst and reliving all of the bad things his boss has said to him. In his imagination, he is feeling the hurt and anger of his boss' transgressions towards him. By the time he gets to the office, Jon is emotionally spent. He is never surprised when his boss has something to say to him that is in line with his mental conversations he has been having.

But here is the TRUTH.

Jon is completely unaware that it is his own mental conversations that are creating the situation. His habitual imaginary conversations are literally producing or attracting their physical equivalent into his life experience.

That's right.

Jon is responsible for all of it.

Here's the good news though; and you're going to like it. There is a simple solution for Jon...

And it works miraculously.

◆◆◆

Jon Works a Miracle

Jon read an incredible book on the Secrets of the Imagination. (lol) :) In it, he learned about his almighty, powerful, imagination. He put some of the techniques to work immediately to change his situation. Here is what he did.

After reading the book, he decided that he needed to radically change his thinking. He wanted to overhaul his imagination. Jon decided to take the Seven Day Ultimate Manifesting Challenge. He spent an entire week changing his imaginal thoughts just to test and see what happened.

For a whole week before going to sleep, he laid in his bed and held a long imaginary conversation with his boss. Unlike former imaginary conversations where his boss was always saying negative things to him, these nightly conversations were very positive.

Each night, Jon imagined his boss saying the most wonderful things to him. Things like "Jon, you're doing a great job." and "Thanks for all of your hard work." He would imagine a friendly, sincere, smile on his boss' face as he spoke to him. Jon would build these mental conversations up in his mind to the point where **he began to feel the mental joy and satisfaction** that would come as if these things were being said in real life.

In his imagination, Jon's boss was praising him for his great work. He could practically feel him patting him on the back. He could see the faces of his coworkers as they overheard him being praised. Jon felt amazing as he indulged in the emotion of being honored and respected. It felt GOOD.

Each evening Jon purposefully feel asleep in this successful mood. In the mornings, he would wake up and immediately try to get right back into the feeling he had before going to bed. Furthermore, as he drove to work, he quit the negative conversations he had been having and replaced them with positive mental conversations. In his mind, he was genuinely smiling at his boss, accepting his praise, shaking his hand, being promoted, etc.

After one week, what do you think happened?

Well, I don't think I need to tell you what happened, because we all know that when you change what's happening inside your imagination, the outside changes too. It's basic Law of Attraction 101. The outside must and always does equal the inside.

The conclusion to Jon's story however, is not what you might have expected.

◆◆◆

What happened to Jon?

On day 4 of his imagination experiment Jon was really beginning to feel great. Things at work seemed better but definitely were not perfect. However, he was really beginning to enjoy his nightly routine of having wonderful conversations with his boss.

The mental exercises were becoming easier and easier to complete. He found that getting into that feeling or mood of being honored and respected by his boss was not difficult to do. He was trusting the process. Then something weird happened.

On the morning of day 5, Jon overslept. He never did that, but on this day, Jon was horribly late for work. When he arrived, his boss called him into the office, yelled at him and fired him.

Jon couldn't believe it. It was so strange to be fired. He had never been fired before; especially by a boss who he was beginning to feel very friendly towards because of his nightly imagination exercises. He was at a loss, but was able to quickly gather himself together and look for another job.

He reached out to some friends and shared his predicament. Thankfully, Jon was able to immediately get a job at another company. The work was a bit different than what he was accustomed to but all the same he gave it a try.

◆◆◆

The Miracle

Jon began working for this new company and found he really enjoyed it. Days turned into weeks, and weeks turned into months and then finally, years. He had "accidentally" found a new career.

When asked what he liked about working for this company, Jon had an easy answer. He highlighted the fact that his boss showed him respect. He also felt valued by his management and his coworkers. He never felt the need to leave because he kept getting promoted and he had been honored on several occasions for his great work.

Sound familiar?

Also...

> *Jon never discontinued his nightly imagination exercises.*

That's right.

- He made it a habit of always going to bed imagining and feeling honored and respected.
- He always imagined himself being promoted and congratulated by his bosses and coworkers.
- He always indulged in the feeling of success as he drifted off to sleep.

You can do the same thing that Jon did.

Start tonight and for seven days take something that you do not like in your life and rewrite it to conform to your own wishes. Watch and see what your almighty, all powerful, imagination will do for you.

"Imagining creates reality."

-Neville Goddard

MAGIC

Magic. What is it? Is it illusion? Is it real? What makes the magician so special and what mysterious powers does he wield that we ordinary human beings are not entitled to? These questions inflame our imagination and haunt our psyche. Our rational mind and our imagination battle each other for the answer.

For hundreds, even thousands of years, magicians have entertained not only the common masses, but Kings and Queens too. Their performances leave us in awe. The ability to make an object disappear or even to create something from thin air has always fascinated us. We watch the magician pull a rabbit out of a hat and he is instantly elevated in our minds; he becomes as a god to us. We want to know how the trick is done.

On the surface, we know there is a logical explanation. Beneath our conscious thinking, however, deep inside, a hidden chord is struck and touches at the very heart of a deep mystery that secretly terrifies us all. The reason human beings feel this way is simple; when you have the Key.

The truth is, we are all magicians of sorts. The powerful inner workings of our minds have all the stuff it takes to pull anything you want out of the proverbial hat. In fact, we all...each of us, are pulling rabbits out of our hats (subconscious minds) all the time, because the thoughts and feelings simmering inside of us are always growing and taking form on the outside in our daily lives.

Stated simply, when our hidden thoughts and feelings pass through the imagination and are ready or subjectified, they pop out of the proverbial hat and into our objective experiences. That is why we know that things don't just happen to us. The outside is simply a result of the magic that has been going on, on the inside.

Stated in another way; our imaginations produce the phenomena of our lives. **We are the magicians**. You may want to pause for a moment and reread the previous sentence. You might even have to catch your breath! This information is shocking if understood correctly.

Again...WE ARE THE MAGICIANS. We are practicing true magic because we have the ability to make our words/imaginings come true.

Once this sinks in, you will of course want to begin to use this knowledge immediately to improve every aspect of your situation in life. You can now begin to pull things out of your hat that are determined by you. The first thing to do is simple. Take control of the thoughts and emotions constantly being released by your mind.

Because you will never stop thinking and feeling, the only choice for you now is to wisely determine your inner life. Every thought released by you has a mysterious creative power wrapped up inside of it. It begins to take shape immediately just as a seed begins to germinate under the soil where no one can see it until one day the tiny seedling pops up out of the ground for all to see (much like pulling a rabbit out of a hat).

We don't know everything about how this power works but we do know that our imagination produces or attracts to us physical things and experiences. In fact, we are so intertwined with the creation of our experiences through the inner workings of our imaginations, that we may say that we are intimately united to the very Creative Power we pray to.

Stated another way: Your imagination is the creative gift of God. Use it wisely and you get everything you want. Used unwisely, you create pain and misery.

In fact, using the imagination is the same as praying.

Stay with me here!

Prayer is a petition to our God. Oftentimes it is a verbal or non-verbal request to the creator to give us some material or spiritual benefit. We pray and according to our faith is it done unto us. Likewise, according to the Law of Attraction: When we imagine/visualize/feel something as true, we are asking for that thing to become a reality.

In this business of manifesting, we know that what we imagine and feel as real, comes to pass. So, when we imagine something, we can say we are "praying" for that thing to happen. You see...we say the prayer...and we answer the prayer; all through the use of the imaginative faculty.

Truly, God (the Creative Power) resides within us.

> *"Neither shall they say, Lo here! Or, lo there! for, behold, the kingdom of God is within you."*
>
> *Luke 17:21*

> *"The soul contains the event that shall befall it; for the event is only the actualization of its thoughts; and what we pray to ourselves for is always granted."*
>
> *-Ralph Waldo Emerson*

THE SOURCE OF PROBLEMS

There is no question that suffering exists in the world. In our communities we find people that are hungry, need jobs, are on drugs, drinking; there are children without parents, etc... The question of how to help society's ills elicits different responses from different people. The worst is when we know someone personally that needs help but we don't know how to provide that help.

◆◆◆

All Things Originate in the Mind

You've read this before. "The inside equals the outside," and "As above, so below." Well...it's true. But most people say it without the gravity that it deserves. Because when it comes to your imagination, we are talking about a powerful tool. What you imagine and feel (inside) becomes a fact in your life (outside). What happens in the Heavens or your Imagination (above), happens in the World (below).

Not only is the imagination a powerful tool, it is a tool that you are intimately linked to. You cannot escape it. The imagination will continue to manifest its' equivalent in your life whether you like it or not. Period.

What does this mean?

It means that we have to become responsible thinkers. We have to recognize our imagination as the creative power that it is and entertain only thoughts and feelings that correspond to what we truly wish for in life. If we don't, we will attract to ourselves whatever thoughts that happen to enter our minds from the outside influences such as television, social media, well meaning friends and family, etc.

To the average person who has not been schooled or initiated into the mysterious secrets of the imagination this sounds a bit crazy, and rightly so. Who could ever imagine that our thoughts create the events of our lives? The point is, when it comes to helping people, we have to start by removing the cause of the problem.

What is the cause? I think we all know the answer to this question by now.

The cause of our problems is most certainly misuse of the imagination. Millions of people are living their lives and unknowingly stuck in a vicious cycle; they imagine terrible things and thereby attract to themselves equivalent problems. They solve those problems, and then go immediately on to create some more. It's awful to watch.

But it's not their fault. Who would guess that worrying about something makes it happen? Who could suspect that being fearful attracts a fearful event? Or conversely, who would ever believe that the feeling of wealth, attracts wealth? Or that indulging in the emotion of love would attract love into one's life?

It's like a terrible joke that the creator has played on us. We get dropped off in this World without a rulebook telling us how the game is played. We have to struggle, and suffer for a while before figuring out how life really works.

But you don't have to suffer anymore! The truth is in your hands now. Congratulations! You have finally discovered the power of your almighty imagination. Now you have the ability to imagine purposefully to create and attract your dream life.

IMAGINATION AND ASTRAL TRAVEL

James had not heard from an old friend in many years. "It's funny how time can pass by so quickly," he thought. It sure would be nice to talk to him and catch up. Desiring to reconnect, he spent some time looking around the house for his telephone number but without any luck.

Later that evening, James sat quietly thinking of some of the good old days and the fun times he used to have with his old pal. While reminiscing, James closed his eyes and drifted off to sleep. He had a vivid dream where he could recall talking in an animated way with his friend. It was a good dream and he woke up the following morning with a sense that they had connected somehow. Then something strange happened.

Later that morning he received a phone call. It was from the very same friend whom he had been thinking and dreaming about the night before! James was very surprised to hear the voice of his buddy on the other end of the line.

Then he said something that shocked him. He actually felt the hair on his arm stand up.

What did he say?

His friend told him that he had had a dream about him the previous night. In the dream, they talked and had a good time. He woke up feeling like it would be nice to call him up and have a chat and that is the reason for the unexpected phone call.

James was simply speechless. He didn't mention that he had had almost exactly the same dream because that would just sound weird. But he couldn't get over it. What a bizarre coincidence he thought to himself. How can two people separated by thousands of miles have the same dream and be in it together?

The answer is simple: Your imagination is not limited by space... or time for that matter.

And don't get hung up here. Don't be scared, but...

Sometimes your dreams are real.

Yes. It's true. You can and do often travel to distant locations while you sleep. The imagination is not limited by distance and can travel anywhere almost instantaneously.

What this means is that when you use your imagination say for instance to think about an old friend and you then imagine talking with that old friend as you fall asleep, don't be surprised if your deeper self does not take a trip at night to go and have a visit.

James, after he got off the phone, sat quietly pondering what had happened. It's true that this was not the first time he had had a dream where he woke up feeling that everything was so real. Most of the time he couldn't understand his dreams and often felt that they were somehow symbolic and were a bunch of mysterious messages from his subconscious mind or something like that.

But sometimes, he definitely had dreams where he either felt like he had been flying or had been interacting with other people and having normal conversations. James had always let these experiences remain a secret. They were just too weird to talk about with normal everyday people. Plus, he rarely met another person who had had similar experiences to share with him.

Then he remembered a strange book that he had found in a used book store years ago. The subject was about dreaming and being able to travel to other places in what is called your dream body or your astral body. After reading it he remembered being so impressed that he immediately went out and found everything that author had ever written. The name of the author was Carlos Castaneda.

James started eagerly rummaging through the bookshelves in his office library. Then he found it. Right there in front of his eyes was his old copy of Carlos Castaneda's The Art of Dreaming. It was all coming back to him now. "I had forgotten this was possible," he thought to himself.

"Who am I going to visit tonight?" He smiled and opened it up to chapter one. :)

SEVEN DAY ULTIMATE CHALLENGE

Congratulations! You've made it to the end. There is one final piece of business to attend to. :)

Obviously you can't just put this book down and expect your life to change. I've learned from personal experience that it's very easy to know the truth yet not put in the work to make any meaningful changes.

We've said it over and over in this book that imagining creates your reality. Now the time has come for you to do something. What I mean by that is that you must take action. My deepest hope is that you will take this information and **develop a definite method of working.**

So my question is this: If the Truth presented here resonates with you, what are you going to do about it? You can change everything…easily, but you have to put in the work of imagining your desired outcome. You have to put yourself in that state or mood of the wish fulfilled and you have to do it *consistently*.

So, that being said; I have a recommendation, or if you will, call it a challenge. Here it is.

◆◆◆

7 Day Ultimate Manifesting Challenge

START NOW. Literally, start right now. As you put this book down, grab a piece of paper and take a few minutes to write down some thing or some situation that if it were now a reality would be really, really great for you. You've read this book to the end so I know you have something in mind already! Put it on paper.

Next, promise yourself that every day for the next seven days you will find 10-15 minutes to go somewhere private and get into the mood or feeling of what it would feel like if this wish has been fulfilled. I don't care if you do this manifesting exercise somewhere during the day or if you wait and do it as you drift off to sleep at night. But you can do both! Just be sure to do it every day!

Prove to yourself once and for all that **life is truly all imagination.**

Finally, share your results with me. When this works for you (and I know it will) I will be thrilled to hear about your success. Drop a line or two on a blog post at my website mentalscientist.com, share it on Facebook, Tweet it out, or email me. Your success is my success and motivates me to write more of this content.

So with that I say Thank you! Good Luck! ...and Happy manifesting!

Many Blessings to you.

Walt

"Indulge the feeling you would have if your miracle came to pass and you too will discover the Secrets of Your Imagination"

Walter Crosson

Thank you for reading!

If you enjoyed this book would you kindly

give it a review on Amazon?

Mental Scientist

Another Book by Walter Crosson:

Twenty-Five Neville Goddard Manifesting Techniques

Find it at mentalscientist.com

54 | SECRETS OF THE IMAGINATION

Printed in Great Britain
by Amazon